Your Smile is Magical

SHARON L. ELAM

FRANKLIN ROSE
PUBLISHING

Publisher: Franklin Rose, Inc.

www.FranklinRose.com

Thank you to my

Beautiful Granddaughters

Amanda and Sara

Who have

Blessed my life,

With three

Great Grandchildren

Harper, Rowly, and Warren

And those yet to join us.

MY DEAREST KATIE
FOR ALL THE
THINGS MY HANDS
HAVE HELD THE
BEST BY FAR
IS YOU.

Inspiration

My inspiration for writing this book is my daughter, Katie, who transitioned from this life to the next on March 7, 2018, one day before her 51st birthday. Katie was born on March 8, 1967.

This book is an insight into a child's unspoken words and feelings toward a loved one.

It describes what a child feels and sees from their eyes and how they experience this new world, they have chosen to become a part of.

It is our reminder and an example of what total unconditional love is all about. Our mission and purpose in this life is to love one another.

Our love connection is from birth when we see our child face to face for the first time.

We fall in love immediately with our newborn child through the miracle of birth.

Another one of God's Masterpieces has been born.

This child has chosen us to become their caregiver, role model, and mentor as they start their life journey.

Katie was the greatest blessing that God has ever given to me.

My dearest Katie, thank you for choosing me and everything you taught me.

I love you for all eternity.

Mom

your smile
is
Magical

Your smile delights me
Your smile makes me
feel warm inside

Your smile
makes me feel loved

Your smile makes me
feel cared about

your smile
is Magical

Your smile tells me

you are *glad* to see me

Your smile tells me
you understand me
when I wiggle my
arms and legs

Your smile tells me
you are happy

when I laugh
and play

your
smile
is
Magical

STORYTIME

Your smile tells me you are
having happy thoughts
about me

Your smile tells me
you care about what
is going on with me

your smile
is
Magical

Your smile lifts
my heart

Your smile gives me

courage to go on

Your smile shares a part
of you with me

your
smile
is
Magical

Your smile gives me
the strength to smile
back at you

So that I can
share a part
of who I am
with who you are

My Prayer
For You

"May the Lord smile on you and
be gracious to you.
May the Lord show you His favour
and give you, His peace."

Numbers 6:25-26

About The Author

Sharon Elam has dedicated over 30 years of her life to the profession of teaching.

Throughout her career, she touched the lives of countless students from diverse age groups, ranging from enthusiastic Kindergartners to two-year Community College students.

A love of learning has been a driving force in Sharon's life for herself and her students.

This passion for knowledge constantly motivates her to seek and uncover the positive side of every learning experience.

She firmly believes that education is a lifelong journey and that the quest for knowledge never ends.

Though Sharon has retired from formal teaching, her enthusiasm for education remains undiminished.

Her most remarkable joy now comes from watching her three Great-Grandchildren embark on their own lifelong learning journeys.

Each step of their development brings her immense happiness, as she knows they are laying the foundations for a bright and promising future.

Throughout her life, Sharon has held a deep faith and belief in God. This spiritual foundation has guided her actions, instilling in her a sense of gratitude and humility.

May God's Blessings and Protection always be with us.

About The Illustrator

Lauren Bulter has worked in the art profession for almost two decades of her life. Exploring various expressions and outlets, from hanging works in galleries to illustration, design, and film. Her passion lies in expression, which touches others.

A student of animation, she finds joy in stories. Stories that allow us to reflect on ourselves, stories that shift our perspective on the world around us and make it anew. Stories that teach, stories that remind us how passionately we feel, stories that heal.

Find Lauren on Facebook or Instagram @LaurelArtAndDesign